THE LITERARY CAT

The
Literary
Cat

RUNNING PRESS
Philadelphia, Pennsylvania

Canadian representatives: General Publishing Co., Ltd., 30 Lesmill Road, Don Mills, Ontario M3B 2T6.

International representatives: Worldwide Media Services, Inc., 115 East Twenty-third Street, New York, New York 10010.

9 8 7 6 5 4 3

Digit on the right indicates the number of this printing.

Library of Congress Cataloging-in-Publication Number 89-62863

ISBN 0-89471-796-0

This book may be ordered by mail from the publisher. Please add $1.00 for postage and handling. *But try your bookstore first!* Running Press Book Publishers 125 South Twenty-second Street Philadelphia, Pennsylvania 19103

Introduction

No wonder the ancient Egyptians worshipped cats as gods—is there an animal with more dignity, more aloof serenity, and innate grandeur? What other domestic creature behaves like an honored guest and is treated as an equal?

Cats fix us with their gaze and put us in our place. They beguile us with their startling affection and charm us with the beauty of their fluid bodies. They amaze us with their composure and delight us with their agility.

Try to capture a cat with a generalization and you will be proven wrong, for cats are mercurial —as swift in mood as they are in movement, playful one moment, elusive the next. Communicative today, reclusive tomorrow, their motivations remain unknowable, yet their presence becomes essential to our lives.

Cats do as they please, and for that we admire—and even revere —them. They treat us as companions, demanding and receiving our respect as their due. The fact that they choose to spend their lives with us is a gift we accept gratefully.

There are no ordinary cats.

COLETTE
French writer

His friendship is not easily won but it is something worth having.

MICHAEL JOSEPH
English publisher

It is impossible for a lover of cats to banish these alert, gentle, and discriminating little friends, who give us just enough of their regard and complaisance to make us hunger for more.

AGNES REPPLIER
American essayist

We cannot, without becoming cats, perfectly understand the cat mind.

ST. GEORGE MIVART
19th-century authority on cats

To understand a cat, you must realize that he has his own gifts, his own viewpoint, even his own morality.

LILIAN JACKSON BRAUN
American writer

The really great thing about cats is their endless variety. One can pick a cat to fit almost any kind of decor, color scheme, income, personality, mood. But under the fur, whatever color it may be, there still lies, essentially unchanged, one of the world's free souls.

ERIC GURNEY
American cartoonist and writer

He lives in the half-lights in secret places, free and alone—this mysterious little-great being whom his mistress calls "My cat."

MARGARET BENSON
English writer

In Ancient Egypt they were worshipped as gods. This makes them too prone to set themselves up as critics and censors of the frail and erring human beings whose lot they share.

P.G. WODEHOUSE
English writer

A sleeping cat
is ever alert.

FRED SCHWAB
American writer

The only mystery about the cat is why it ever decided to become a domestic animal.

SIR COMPTON MACKENZIE
English writer

No tame animal has lost less of its native dignity or maintained more of its ancient reserve. The domestic cat might rebel tomorrow.

WILLIAM CONWAY
Archbishop of Armagh

The cat, like the genius, draws into itself as into a shell except in the atmosphere of congeniality, and this is the secret of its remarkable and elusive personality.

IDA M. MELLEN
American writer

The cat is mighty
dignified until the dog
comes by.

SOUTHERN FOLK SAYING

Who can believe that
there is no soul behind
those luminous eyes!

THEOPHILE GAUTIER
French writer and critic

No heaven will not ever
Heaven be
Unless my cats are there
to welcome me.

The smallest feline is a masterpiece.

LEONARDO DA VINCI
Italian artist

My little grandson is a
darling, but he can never
take the place of my cats.

ANONYMOUS AMERICAN
GRANDMOTHER

In Egypt, the cats . . . afford evidence that animal nature is not altogether intractable, but that when well-treated they are good at remembering kindness.

AELIAN
Roman writer

The Cat was a creature of absolute convictions, and his faith in his deductions never varied.

MARY E. WILKINS FREEMAN
American writer

Some Cats is blind,
and stone-deaf some,
But ain't no Cat
wuz ever dumb.

ANTHONY HENDERSON EUWER
American poet and writer

One of the most striking differences between a cat and a lie is that a cat has only nine lives.

MARK TWAIN
American writer

The cat seldom interferes with other people's rights. His intelligence keeps him from doing many of the fool things that complicate life.

CARL VAN VECHTEN
American writer and photographer

There are people who reshape the world by force or argument, but the cat just lies there, dozing, and the world quietly reshapes itself to suit his comfort and convenience.

ALLEN and IVY DODD
American writers

At dinner time he would sit in a corner, concentrating, and suddenly they would say, "Time to feed the cat," as if it were their own idea.

LILIAN JACKSON BRAUN
American writer

"**Me**ow" is like "Aloha"—
it can mean anything.

HANK KETCHUM
American cartoonist

Cats seem to go on the principle that it never does any harm to ask for what you want.

JOSEPH WOOD KRUTCH
American writer

If man could be crossed
with the cat, it would
improve man but
deteriorate the cat.

MARK TWAIN
American writer

With the qualities of cleanliness, affection, patience, dignity, and courage that cats have, how many of us, I ask you, would be capable of becoming cats?

FERNAND MERY
French writer

No self-respecting cat
wants to be an artist's
model.

The trouble with cats is that they've got no tact.

P.G. WODEHOUSE
English writer

If you want to be a psychological novelist and write about human beings, the best thing you can do is keep a pair of cats.

ALDOUS HUXLEY
English writer

If a cat does something, we call it instinct; if we do the same thing, for the same reason, we call it intelligence.

WILL CUPPY
American writer

—⬥—

Way down deep, we're
all motivated by the
same urges. Cats have
the courage to live
by them.

JIM DAVIS
American cartoonist

Tobermory looked squarely at her for a moment and then fixed his gaze serenely on the middle distance. It was obvious that boring questions lay outside his scheme of life.

SAKI (Hector Hugh Munro)
English writer

Even overweight cats
instinctively know the
cardinal rule: when fat,
arrange yourself in
slim poses.

JOHN WEITZ
American designer

Sometimes the veil between human and animal intelligence wears very thin—then one experiences the supreme thrill of keeping a cat, or perhaps allowing oneself to be owned by a cat.

CATHERINE MANLEY
English writer

Cats, like men,
are flatterers.

WILLIAM S. LANDOR
English poet

God made the cat in order that man might have the pleasure of caressing the lion.

FERNAND MERY
French writer

A dog is a dog, a bird is a bird, and a cat is a person.

MUGSY PEABODY
American writer

A dog, I have always said, is prose; a cat is a poem.

JEAN BURDEN
American writer

If a fish is the movement of water embodied, given shape, then a cat is a diagram and pattern of subtle air.

DORIS LESSING
English writer

Nothing is so difficult as to paint the cat's face, which as Moncrif justly observes, bears a character of "finesse and hilarity."

CHAMPFLEURY
(Jules Fleury-Husson)
French writer

There is nothing in the animal world, to my mind, more delightful than grown cats at play. They are so swift and light and graceful, so subtle and designing, and yet so richly comic.

MONICA EDWARDS
English writer

The best exercise for a
cat is another cat.

JO and PAUL LOEB
*American animal trainers and
writers*

No matter how much cats fight, there always seem to be plenty of kittens.

ABRAHAM LINCOLN
U.S. President

It is a very inconvenient habit of kittens (Alice had once made the remark) that, whatever you say to them, they always purr.

LEWIS CARROLL
English writer

A kitten is so flexible that she is almost double; the hind parts are equivalent to another kitten with which the forepart plays. She does not discover that her tail belongs to her until you tread on it.

HENRY DAVID THOREAU
American writer

A kitten is the most irresistible comedian in the world. Its wide-open eyes gleam with wonder and mirth. It darts madly at nothing at all, and then, as though suddenly checked in the pursuit, prances sideways on its hind legs with ridiculous agility and zeal.

AGNES REPPLIER
American essayist

Four little Persians, but one only looked in my direction. I extended a tentative finger and two soft paws clung to it. There was a contented sound of purring, I suspect on both our parts.

GEORGE FREEDLEY
American writer

Nothing's more playful than a young cat, nor more grave than an old one.

THOMAS FULLER
English writer and preacher

It is, of course, totally pointless to call a cat when it is intent on the chase. They are deaf to the interruptive nonsense of humans. They are on cat business, totally serious and involved.

JOHN D. MacDONALD
American writer

A cat sleeps fat, yet walks thin.

FRED SCHWAB
American writer

He shut his eyes while Saha (the cat) kept vigil, watching all the invisible signs that hover over sleeping human beings when the light is put out.

COLETTE
French writer

Cats are a mysterious kind of folk. There is more passing in their minds than we are aware of.

SIR WALTER SCOTT
English writer

Give her but a wavering leaf-shadow of a breeze combing the grasses and she was back a million years, glaring with night-lit eyes in the thickets, projecting a terrible aura of fear that stilled and quelled all creatures.

PAUL ANNIXTER
American writer

Because of our willingness to accept cats as superhuman creatures, they are the ideal animals with which to work creatively.

RONI SCHOTTER
American writer

Women, poets, and especially artists, like cats; delicate natures only can realize their sensitive nervous systems.

HELEN M. WINSLOW
American writer

As an inspiration to the author, I do not think the cat can be over-estimated. He suggests so much grace, power, beauty, motion, mysticism. I do not wonder that many writers love cats; I am only surprised that all do not.

CARL VAN VECHTEN
American writer and photographer

Stately, kindly, lordly
friend condescend
Here to sit by me,
and turn
Glorious eyes that smile
and burn . . . .

ALGERNON CHARLES
SWINBURNE
English poet

—

You could never accuse him of idleness, and yet he knew the secret of repose.

CHARLES DUDLEY WARNER
American writer

The cat is a dilettante in fur.

THEOPHILE GAUTIER
French writer and critic

Cats everywhere asleep
on the shelves like
motorized bookends.

AUDREY THOMAS
American/Canadian writer

Purring would seem to be, in her case, an automatic safety-valve device for dealing with happiness overflow.

MONICA EDWARDS
English writer

I wish you could see the two cats drowsing side by side in a Victorian nursing chair, their paws, their ears, their tails complementally adjusted, their blue eyes blinking open on a single thought of when I shall remember it's their suppertime. They might have been composed by Bach for two flutes.

SYLVIA TOWNSEND WARNER
English writer

Cats are rather delicate
creatures and they are
subject to a good many
ailments, but I never
heard of one who
suffered from insomnia.

JOSEPH WOOD KRUTCH
American writer

A little drowsing cat
is an image
of perfect beatitude.

CHAMPFLEURY
(Jules Fleury-Husson)
French writer

He loved books, and when he found one open on the table he would lie down on it, turn over the edges of the leaves with his paw, and, after a while, fall asleep, for all the world as if he had been reading a fashionable novel.

THEOPHILE GAUTIER
French writer and critic

In a cat's eyes,
all things belong to cats.

ENGLISH PROVERB

The tail, of course, must come forward until it reaches the front paws. Only an inexperienced kitten would let it dangle.

LLOYD ALEXANDER
American writer

Although all cat games have their rules and ritual, these vary with the individual player. The cat, of course, never breaks a rule. If it does not follow precedent, that simply means it has created a new rule and it is up to you to learn it quickly if you want the game to continue.

SIDNEY DENHAM
English writer

The cat is never vulgar.

CARL VAN VECHTEN
American writer and photographer

If he had asked to have the door opened, and was eager to go out, he always went deliberately; I can see him now, standing on the sill, looking about at the sky as if he was thinking whether it were worth while to take an umbrella.

MARGARET BENSON
English writer

A cat, our new Maine friends claimed, is always on the wrong side of the door.

ALLEN and IVY DODD
American writers

Cats know how to obtain food without labor, shelter without confinement, and love without penalties.

W.L. GEORGE
American writer

To please himself only
the cat purrs.

IRISH PROVERB

It is remarkable, in cats, that the outer life they reveal to their masters is one of perpetual confident boredom.

ROBLEY WILSON, JR.
American writer

For push of nose, for perseverance, there is nothing to beat a cat.

EMILY CARR
Canadian painter and writer

No matter how tired or wretched I am, a pussy-cat sitting in a doorway can divert my mind.

MARY E. WILKINS FREEMAN
American writer

The cat is, above all things, a dramatist.

MARGARET BENSON
English writer

Honest as the cat when the meat is out of reach.

ENGLISH PROVERB

Cats have a contempt of speech. Why should they talk when they can communicate without words?

LILIAN JACKSON BRAUN
American writer

Never ask a hungry cat whether he loves you for yourself alone.

DR. LOUIS J. CAMUTI
American veterinarian

Nobody who is not prepared to spoil cats will get from them the reward they are able to give to those who do spoil them.

SIR COMPTON MACKENZIE
English writer

I love cats because I enjoy my home; and little by little, they become its visible soul.

JEAN COCTEAU
French poet and filmmaker

For every house is incompleat without him, and a blessing is lacking in the spirit.

CHRISTOPHER SMART
English poet

What fun to be a cat!

CHRISTOPHER MORLEY
American writer

Cats love one so much—
more than they will allow.
But they have so much
wisdom they keep it to
themselves.

MARY E. WILKINS FREEMAN
American writer

RUNNING PRESS Miniature Editions™

Aesop's Fables
As A Man Thinketh
A Child's Garden of Verses
Emily Dickinson: Selected Poems
Friendship: A Bouquet of Quotes
The Literary Cat
Love: Quotations from the Heart
Quotable Women
Sherlock Holmes: Two Complete Adventure
Sonnets from the Portuguese
The Velveteen Rabbit

This book has been bound using handcraf
methods, and Smythe-sewn to ensure
durability.

The dust jacket was designed by Toby
Schmidt and illustrated by Mimi Vang Olser
The interior was designed by Judith Barbou
Osborne and illustrated by Naomi Kurz.
The text was set in American Classic by
Commcor Communications Corporation,
Philadelphia, Pennsylvania.